A Change of Heart

Also by Randy Blasing

POETRY

Sweet Crude
Choice Words: Poems 1970-2005
Second Home
Graphic Scenes
The Double House of Life
The Particles
To Continue
Light Years

SELECTED TRANSLATIONS (with Mutlu Konuk)

Poems of Nazim Hikmet
Human Landscapes from My Country:
    An Epic Novel in Verse by Nazim Hikmet
Letters to Taranta-Babu: A Poem by Nazim Hikmet

A Change of Heart

poems

Randy Blasing

Copper Beech Press
Providence

Grateful acknowledgment is made to the editors of *The Yale Review,* where "Portents," "Summer Evening in New England," and "Albuquerque Aubade" first appeared.

Cover painting by KL Martel
Author photograph by Tezer Orhan

Copyright 2018 by Randy Blasing

All rights reserved.
For information, address the publisher:
Copper Beech Press
POB 2578
Providence, RI 02906
www.copperbeechpress@yahoo.com
Library of Congress Control Number: 2018962243

Publisher's Cataloging-in-Publication Data
(Prepared by The Donohue Group, Inc.)
Names: Blasing, Randy, author.
Title: A change of heart : poems / Randy Blasing.
Description: First edition. | Providence, [Rhode Island] : Copper
    Beech Press, [2018] | Some poems previously published in the
Yale Review.
Identifiers: ISBN 9780914278863 | ISBN 091427886X
Subjects: LCSH: Blasing, Randy–Poetry. | Near-death experiences–
    Poetry. | Heart-surgery–Poetry. | Spiritual life–Poetry.
 Classification: LCC PS3552.L38 C43 2018 | DDC 811/.54–dc23

ISBN 13: 978-0-914278-86-3
ISBN 10: 0-914278-86-X

Set in Perpetua
Printed by Stillwater River Publications
Manufactured in the United States of America
First Edition

for Kerri Lee
& *my* boys, John & Ezra,
who saw me through hell

Harrow the house of the dead; look shining at
New styles of architecture, a change of heart.
W. H. Auden

CONTENTS

I

Spring Triptych   *11*
Easter, 1960   *14*
Words for My Ex-Mother-in-Law   *15*
Continuing Education   *16*
Memorial Day, 2015   *17*
Piece Work   *18*
Color Lines   *19*
Yo   *20*
Home by Morning   *21*
Lavender Season on Route 66   *23*
Numbers   *24*
To an Old Friend Whose Work Has Come to Something   *25*
Summer Evening in New England   *26*
Living History   *27*
River Road   *28*
Dark Horse   *29*
Richard Avedon at the Peabody   *30*
Personal Days   *31*
Almost Amherst   *32*
Portents   *33*

II

Pre-Op   *37*
Code Blue   *38*
Albuquerque Aubade   *39*
Near Death   *40*
Dead-End Pre-Med   *41*
The Life Saver   *42*
Like New   *43*
Heart Failure   *44*
Norwegian Eyes   *45*
One in a Million   *46*
End Zone   *47*
Breakfast with Jerome   *48*
Another Day in Paradise   *49*
Worlds Apart   *50*
Homesick for Here   *51*
Late Revelation   *52*
Welcome to Asia   *53*
The Snow Man   *61*
February Is for the Birds   *62*
Hard Spring   *64*

I

SPRING TRIPTYCH

1. Holding Hands in Recovery

The creep who cut you first but left you septic
stood by & watched you die all day, until
only a miracle could rescue you.

Tonight, when you transitioned from the OR
to Intensive Care, I took your hand as if
guiding you back, I hoped, from death to life,

your big eyes green & wide but sadly un-
comprehending, like Bambi's at the end.
Stranded between the living & the dead

to the world, you couldn't tell if you'd return
to this place where everybody kept asking
the same dumb-ass question: *Are you in pain?*

Of course you were (& are), though you can't feel
anything anymore, your tears written off
as symptoms of dry eyes. Feeling's a pain.

2. Hospital Blues

Did he do this to me? you wondered, seeing
the man in blue—"Dr. Philosophy"—
standing at the foot of your bed this morning.

Yesterday, when I asked you if you wanted
anything, you answered with your first breath
on your own there in the ICU: *I want*

to die. Today you couldn't stop crying,
staring at your future in your mind,
because you couldn't face it. For weeks I'd sat

& watched your numbers flashing on the screens
above you, like a sleepless Keno player
dead-set on beating the odds in the end.

Now you want to take up your pallet
& walk—a small miracle, given where
you found yourself a short lifetime ago

3. Still Life

It's been forever since you felt the light
of day unmediated by the glass

a black turkey vulture flattened itself
against this morning, its breast & wings spread

across the window of the hospital
you search for evidence of songbirds now,

it being spring today—at least on paper.
Last week they gave you a one-in-three shot

at coming off of life support alive
& thus of living to see this day, confined

(though you remain) to a hospital bed here
& tethered still to a mess of tubes & wires.

Absent songbirds to hail your resurrection,
I made you this little, all-too-human song.

EASTER, 1960

The first Easter I could drive, I borrowed
my father's '58 Fairlane & trans-
ported my grandmother to Crystal Lake
after brunch after church. Down on her hands

& knees at my grandfather's grave she lost
no time finding, she attacked the grass
burying his stone flush with the earth
& brushed it clean of dirt. Helping her stand,

I followed her until, as if sleep-walking,
she stumbled across her forever-thirteen
Elsie's marker she had gone in circles

searching for, buying time to still awake
from her nightmare & keep her first daughter
alive awhile in living memory.

WORDS FOR MY EX-MOTHER-IN-LAW

This March she won't air-mail a pink plum blossom
from Izmir to her daughter in Chicago,
telegraphing her loss without a word,
as she did fifty springs ago. A stroke

has left her speechless, whose words once cascaded
from her Black Sea Circassian's tongue in every
register but bird-like Istanbulese.
Hilarious & profane both, her speech

lost nothing in translation, where I had
to follow her because the breakneck speed
of her delivery always just escaped
my sadly lifelong hit-or-miss Turkish.

The last time she happened, after ten years,
to hear me speak to her, she broke down, silenced
by tears as I'd be now, hearing the news,
if not for writing, for which she had no use.

CONTINUING EDUCATION

> *The woods are lovely, dark and deep,*
> *But I have promises to keep,*
> *And miles to go before I sleep,*
> *And miles to go before I sleep.*
> Robert Frost

She dropped her pants inside the elevator
that brought us two back to earth from class
last night, & as if blinded by the glare

of her pulled-down tights, I ran a finger down
the first of four lines newly inked in block
letters high on her left thigh. Seeing her bare-

bottomed, I understood how hard her artist
had to concentrate, given his location,
on leaving out a comma after *dark*.

(She knew the lines by heart, she said, because
they'd turned her life around the night she learned
to read them right.) Now her naked body

reminds her every day she is alive
never to try & take her life again.

MEMORIAL DAY, 2015

> . . . an American flag flew from a single tall
> pole like a signal of decency and goodness.
> James Salter

All the neighborhood vets behave themselves
as they hardly did while alive, remaining

in place & keeping their hands to themselves, row
after row of draftees as quiet as though

observing en masse a moment of silence
that never ends. Even the little flags

my newly minted Tenderfoot duly
plants in their memory on this blue day

don't make a sound waving in the cool breeze
that drives me from the shade into the sun.

Their headstones, still standing at attention,
tell anyone who wants to know nothing

more than their names & rank; they didn't live
to see the day their life stories fell

as flat as the dashes chiseled in between
their birth & death dates, now carved in granite,

above the bottom line of their time here:
Vietnam, World War I or *II, Korea.*

PIECE WORK

My whole generation has lost their marbles;
mine, for instance, used to hang from the knob

behind the door to my room, stashed as they were
in my dad's white laundry bag—the little

he had to show, not counting the dusty
Purple Heart he showed no interest in,

for four years on a series of destroyers
he'd called home all the way from Midway Island

to Okinawa, where a kamikaze
scoring a direct hit on his stateroom

ran his pants up the ship's mast, broadcasting
his serial number & pronouncing him

missing in action, or worse, on my mother's
radio, his sea chest of treasures deep-sixed.

Those marbles all the colors of my days
of peace his years at war afforded me

are my own souvenirs lost to the world
but found, like him, here in my memory.

COLOR LINES

Our boy called me out as a "brown egg"
when you're a "white." *My* mother got my Welsh

grandfather's olive complexion she passed
on to me from the Spanish whose armada

sank off Wales, & when the survivors thrashed
ashore, in time they mixed their blood from North

Africa with that of the fair-haired locals,
giving rise to the "black" Welsh of south Wales.

My blue-eyed, blond Norwegian grandmother
didn't leave a mark on my mother, who stayed

tan throughout those Minnesota winters
without recourse to Florida or sun lamps.

I tan overnight myself, while my pale-faced
German-English father burned in no time.

I see a pattern in my family tree:
light skin calls unto dark, & vice versa.

YO

"Yo, that's the plate I want!" went a twenty-
something footing it past my car who'd spotted
the four-letter word spelled out in black

& white on my first-ever vanity plate:
POET. What could I say but ask him to wait
until I meet my end, when it will hit

the market again, back in circulation
for him to snag like a carousel's brass ring,
the prize I'd watched for myself before I ran

out of time. That's the story of my life:
keeping time with my heart as long as I can
& now, for good measure, telling the world.

HOME BY MORNING

for Jim Gallegos

My trail to Albuquerque began with cars
my mother started buying me at four
whenever she walked me to our "little store"

on the south side of Minneapolis,
where I first saw toy cars in little yellow
boxes soon to be known as "Matchboxes."

Because I could name every make on sight,
I craved a model of each one. My father
out of town—"on the road," he called it—two

or three weeks at a time, those miniatures
my mother got me must have seemed as close
as she would come to grasping her distant dream

of a "second" car. Years down the road now,
collectors (my fourteen-year-old included)
have gathered here to offer up my past

in vehicles that take me back to it
& make it present, like a sea-foam "Singer"
panel van that speaks to me, its name

still in orange on one side, & recalls
my mother sewing to her heart's content
on her machine or singing her heart out,

live on the radio or in the choir,
much as I've come to stitch together words
I put my heart into & sing this way.

LAVENDER SEASON ON ROUTE 66

I couldn't see, for all the honeybees
gorging themselves on it, the lavender
you found blooming on the side of the road,
nor could I hear the grooved black asphalt hum
"America the Beautiful" embedded
in it once but since worn down, like a '50s
45, when you drove over it
at forty-five in our Dollar Fiesta.

In my day the "Mother Road," it got eaten
(long before your time) by its young—interstates
that, leaving in the dust a local roadside
attraction like the humble lavender,
paved the way for (spare me!) a "global village,"
a monstrosity neither here nor there.

NUMBERS

The summer I turned eight, my family
of three moved into our third house. Our last,
it occupied a hill outside the City
of Lakes in Golden Valley, where I felt
closer than ever to the sky I thought
fell on Chicken Little-me one morning
it lowered the boom—a *sonic* boom, in fact—
as I stepped into the day: a thunder-clap
out of the clear blue had rattled our windows
& left me shaken. Unseen fighter jets
I never saw coming until they'd gone
from sight went & shattered the sound barrier.

Come fall, my father dropped me off downtown
one Saturday to see a matinee
at the Orpheum, a black-&-white movie
about breaking said barrier. The pilot
took a nosedive in his Starfighter,
outrunning sound by riding gravity,
& shook—face changed to Jell-O—like my mental
next-door neighbor I couldn't watch them give
another shock treatment at Glenwood Hills.
In time I turned to numbers, as of beats
per measure, & began flying, as now,
into the future at the speed of sound.

TO AN OLD FRIEND WHOSE WORK HAS COME TO SOMETHING

for Samim

Our paths crossed after I branched out from singing
myself, so to speak, to putting my English
at Nazim Hikmet's service (words my bread-
&-butter) & gave voice to him in Royce Hall
at Turkish Night. In time I bought, for a song,

a summer place in Turkey where, it happened,
you vacationed from CERN, & though I'd followed
particle physics in the *Bulletin
of Atomic Scientists* since high school,
you & I found ourselves on different pages.

Yet we spoke the same language, insofar
as the work we both did—mine on paper,
yours in theory—seemed an end in itself,
for all practical purposes, until
everything unfolded as if by design:

the "God particle" you knew from the get-go
your numbers said existed got "discovered"
at last, while my so-called numbers, these humble
syllables sounding off on time down each line,
still count for nothing in the eyes of the world.

SUMMER EVENING IN NEW ENGLAND

> *To hear an Oriole sing*
> *May be a common Thing*
> *Or only a divine.*
>   Emily Dickinson

Before the katydids did what they do,
serenading their lady loves nightly
& leaving my ears ringing like a buzz-saw,
or, later, the crickets began ticking off

the seconds to the end of summer, the air
fell quiet as the calm between breaths held
while listening for an oriole, the early
evening as cool & sweet as orange sherbet.

The lawn lay at my feet, as flat & brownish
green as the nearby Atlantic at low tide,
in what should have been my fiftieth summer
passed swimming in the incomparable

Aegean & translating into English
the ancient world there, but at this late hour
I must get used to loving summer here
where I will spend forever, starting now.

LIVING HISTORY

for Jim Glickman

Not half a mile up Great Road from the "Half-
House," my home since 9/11, musket
shots echo down it, re-enacting Rhode
Island's War of Independence battle
at Chase Farm—enemy territory

in my own backyard! I wonder if
my neighbors, who still have nothing to say
to me, have it in their hearts after all
to stand their ground locally now & fight
getting screwed over royally by loyal

globalists, as one in three colonists once
risked losing their lives at the hands of world-
famous English cutlery, bayonets
that executed the Redcoats' *coups de grace*
& saved spending any more precious shot

on mere raggle-taggle Americans . . .
Although a good two centuries have passed
since the two brothers building my house fell
out in the middle & left it half-finished,
school children here learn its name to this day.

RIVER ROAD

The moon, a night away from being full,
defies gravity, rising through the sky
at dusk tonight as if lighter than air,
& stays abreast of me, floating as though
weightless on the still Blackstone—a white
peach blossom in an ancient Chinese poem
kissing spring good-bye instead of autumn.

March, November—it comes to the same thing.
The trees anatomized, bare bones one way
or the other, & time gotten out of hand
again as always: *Where on earth did it go?*
The skeletal remains of summer all
remind me how few seasons I have left
to beat the darkness home, dogged by the moon.

DARK HORSE

(Election Day)

The chestnut filly down the road from me—
grazing, as she was, among a flock
of lambs like balls of fog caught on the grass,
heads rooted in the ground—gracefully put

her best foot forward, ankles (as it were)
so thin she hardly seemed to graze the earth,
as if she were above testing the waters
(so to speak) by dipping—what?—a toe

in the dew? She floated in the pasture there,
body & soul all but aloft as I
blew past in my car today, my heart

as light as if I'd taken flight this morning
on the wings of a horse again, giving thanks
as always for the blessings of this country.

RICHARD AVEDON AT THE PEABODY

The un-assassinated President
sat for head shots with his china-doll wife
who, to all appearances a child
herself, kept their newborn's head from rolling

off her shoulder. Nobody knew it then,
but the high point of their lives came in *Look,*
where you first showed these pictures only now
on exhibit because all too soon no one

could bear to see them as you did. JFK
blinked once or twice, as if trying to wake
from the nightmare that history had in mind

for him. Meanwhile, your shutter clicked away,
& he stared into space again, unblinking,
his life flashing still before your eyes.

PERSONAL DAYS

Just a day away from one more Thanksgiving,
I saw the full moon snow my backyard under
when I pulled down the shade on my bedroom
window, preparing to lay me down again.

Ten days ago my mother had been gone
thirty years since the Friday night I lay
in bed, watching *Dallas,* & got the call
that she had died that morning in Orlando.

As for my father, come Valentine's Day
he'll have been missing for as long as he lived,
& I remember walking, his flag in hand,

back from his grave through the everlasting snow
underfoot, bereft even of my own
shadow, sunny though that dark day was.

ALMOST AMHERST

*. . . drifted deep, in Parian, the Village lies—
today,* my sense of it revised, seeing
as it's been turned into a ghost town
by the blizzard that stormed it overnight
with winds that sounded, minus all the bells
& whistles, like its nightly traffic-stopping

freight train. My little world whited out,
as if it's nothing but a mistake in need
of correction, my eyes can't gain a foothold
on what I know by heart but now find changed
to an ancient Greek ruin of white marble.
For all I know, I've woken at the bottom
of my upended snow globe from my childhood
I'm hanging onto by this thread of words.

PORTENTS

> *The knowing glance from star to star . . .*
> James Merrill

I
Sometimes, on a clear night in the middle
of January, the temperature slipping
into the single digits as if counting
down to zero like my body clock,
I watch the other planets circle, bright-
eyed & bushy-tailed, as though closing in
on the earth because they smell blood & sense

it's on its last legs. Meanwhile, all the stars
in the blackened sky get in my eyes & burn
like the distant fires of cities gone up
in smoke at the end of the world, or just
of desert camps indifferent to the certain
doom I feel in my bones as I take out
the trash of one more week of one year less.

II
Carrying out the trash again at one
　—the night as many hours into tomorrow
as my thermometer reads the air is
degrees below zero—I catch my breath
the gift of another January takes
away, here & there the hard stares of planets
asking me what business I have still
standing out in the cold, still above ground.

This year I will surpass my mother's days
on earth, as I did my father's long ago.
When I, like them, come to nothing in time,
their memories will vanish like my breath
going up in smoke against the stars
I see through tears the cold brings to my eyes.

II

PRE-OP

for my mother, Mary, who was all heart

> *I want my feet to be bare,*
> *I want my face to be shaven, and my heart—*
> *you can't plan on the heart, but*
> *the better part of it, my poetry, is open.*
>   Frank O'Hara

Forty years ago in Florida,
the day I climbed Mt. Baldy in the San
Gabriel Mountains & got short of breath

in the thinning air, my mother could have breathed
her last in the OR at Orange Memorial
while undergoing the same open-heart

operation I'm in line for, all thanks
to the heart—damaged, as it proved, from birth—
that I inherited from her. Post-op,

she landed in the psych ward, so far gone
in the head they found her incompetent,
until I had her shrink sort out her meds

& she turned right around, her old self back,
& lived the full seven extra years
her valve-replacement granted her. Like her,

I couldn't help following my heart;
I'm married to it, for better or for worse.
Take care, good doctor, with this mother's son.

CODE BLUE

for Mike Braziller

No sooner did I escape open-heart
surgery with my life than I awoke,
out of the blue, to my heart going *boom*
& lowering the boom, knocking me out

to the point—I'm told—I coded four times,
& four times the nurses on duty gave me
the shock of my life when they zapped me back
to their side of the line I kept crossing

over as they watched. A living, breathing
miracle in the end, I called at last
today to say I finally got released
into the blue June weather color-coded,

by your lights, in my favor for a change,
into rehab as I am, my story
remaining to be written, in your eyes,
the road to recovery my blue road of ink.

ALBUQUERQUE AUBADE

Making a pilgrimage to Albuquerque
to give thanks I cheated heart surgery
of a bad outcome only last month,
I woke my first morning there when the sun,
breaking over Sandia Peak down range
from the Blood of Christ Mountains, targeted me
high in the Marriott, singling me out

to look in the eye. Still asleep, you lay
next to me in bed again, your body
coming back to me in the early light:
I spotted, below your left knee, the skin
you wear my heart on, your life-size tattoo
of it drawn, crisscrossed with black-on-white blood
vessels, from Dr. Fitton's working pictures

of it. I no sooner raised my head
than my nose bled—hadn't I already
lost blood enough, under the knife?—until,
waking in the gloom, you extended me
a mini-tampon smaller than my pinky.
Your tampon up my nose, blood on my hands,
I fell back & wondered what my heart had planned.

NEAR DEATH

There I stood, on the verge of Paradise,
but in my heart I wanted to stay *here,*
as the faces of my loved ones—my boys
& you—all passed before my eyes for, what,

one last time? Whoever's presence I felt
but never saw granted my heart's desire,
& the scene I witnessed flashed back to me
in Santa Fe when I stood face-to-face

with O'Keeffe's *Clouds, 5*: sunrise-gold below
an azure band above a silver line
dividing this world & the next I'd climbed
her gray diagonals of clouds toward.

Instead of crossing over to where visions
like hers in her museum couldn't speak
to me with the power of the Bible's old
handwriting on the wall, I came home to time.

DEAD-END PRE-MED

My heart surgery didn't go as planned:
just when I appeared to be in the clear,

I turned out to be in mortal peril,
losing the beat before a pacemaker

straightened me out. Though I remember standing
at death's door, so to speak, I don't remember

trying—or so I have been told—to assist
the doctors frantic to save my life, the way

(I was also told) my dying father tried,
at the end, to help his doctors find his pulse.

Though I alone survived to tell his story,
I hope he comes alive a moment here

in this deathbed scene I missed, where my would-be-
doctor father lost his only patient.

THE LIFE SAVER

After I got my heart ripped out of me,
it took my body twenty units of blood
to be made whole again, I only learned
two months after the fact. Until then,

you couldn't bear to say what happened, having
cried all the way home after seeing me come
so close to bleeding out, & still I hadn't
made it out of the woods you plunged through, in fact,

into the night. You couldn't yet revisit
the end that didn't come but nearly did
again two days later, as though my life
was fated to be lost. Meanwhile, I found

God but feared I would never be forgiven
for putting you on the same footing of love

LIKE NEW

My new pacemaker, bulging from my chest
(the Cadillac, you said, of such devices)
like a third breast (without, of course, a nipple),
reminds me how, after dying four times,
I came back to life for good finally:
it put my rebuilt heart on cruise control,
keeping it beating now a steady eighty
(no longer miles an hour but beats per minute).

My pulse slowed to a high-end normal rate,
my heart stopped skipping through my days, jumping
out of my chest into my throat, & soon
felt as regular as my old blank-verse
measures my blood (new, too) pulsed through once more
in the small orange notebook you handed me,
my first day in rehab, with the blue pen
I learned cursive with all over again.

HEART FAILURE

for Emily

She helped my heart across the finish line
of the fiftieth & last year I taught.
I got winded trying to read lines out
loud to the end, but she who'd stitched together
in San Francisco, once, a paper dress
composed of lines from "Howl" still managed,
without missing a beat, to start where shortness
of breath had stopped me. Without fail she carried
the day, along with my books (Bishop, Frost)
back to my office after class each week.

After my touch-&-go heart operation
that let me catch my breath, her endless smile
was still there, even as she waved good-bye
for good, it turned out, from her topless white
Cabriolet littered with bumper stickers
that papered over her whole car. She loved
oceanic mammals, but they came down
to paper, too: *Moby-Dick* spoke to her
like nothing else. Gone, she remains as real
on paper, thank you, as my broken heart.

NORWEGIAN EYES

for my student Ashley

After a sudden lapse in the heretofore
scary updates e-mailed her on my heart
surgery last summer, she'd searched the obits

for me, she had to confess when I flashed
before her eyes there in the dying light
of the fall equinox today, but then

when she went & hugged me as if to see
whether I felt as real as I appeared,
I came to life, no ghost now but skin & bones.

As a matter of fact, she said I smelled good
who'd risen from the dead, she learned, in the flesh.
Her eyes flared fjord-blue at the sight of me.

ONE IN A MILLION

The last honeybee of the season cruises
the blue hydrangeas in the pot you left
outside to flourish in fresh air, you hoped,

& full sun. Here it is, the next-to-last
day of September, my all-time favorite month,
the sky the chill blue of heart-stopping eyes.

Your—& my father's—birthday coming up
next month, I owe my life to him & you,
who saw me (& my own failing heart)
through the harrowing events my good doctor

sweated those first days of summer. You watched
over me as I prayed to God & you
at once, facing the same one-in-a-million
chance of living my father had of dying.

END ZONE

(Ollie's Diner)

> *. . . the small delights*
> *Of coffee and a newspaper . . .*
> John Koethe

I start every day I can with a cup
of coffee (black), a bowl of oatmeal dusted
with cinnamon, & a crisp morning paper
nobody reads anymore, I'm afraid,

& in this manner I get squared away,
perceiving all-too clearly where I stand,
going forward, by seating myself here
with both elbows on the table. Forgetting

my manners for the first time in my life,
I live in my own little world, my head
& heart seeing eye-to-eye in the face
of what I have left, give or take a day.

BREAKFAST WITH JEROME

On his first morning in his first home, rescued
yesterday all the way from Arkansas,
I didn't go out but stayed in for breakfast.

Before I'd even touched my Quaker Oats,
he wolfed down his Iams the second they plinked
into his dish like rain on a tin roof.

Who could blame him, though, when he had landed
by chance today on the gravy train of love,
this brown-&-tan German shepherd-Lab puppy

I named after an almost-ghost town
in Arizona saved, too, on the brink
of going under when its copper mine

went bust. Now it's on top of the world, booming
in fact & in its namesake's copper coat.

ANOTHER DAY IN PARADISE

> *Goodness existed; that was the new knowledge.*
> W. H. Auden

If not here, where? I would have said before
I died & stood a step away from heaven
(to my amazement), only to stop short
of crossing the line between here & there.

Turning my back on such peace as I'd never
believed existed anywhere, I wanted
to live for love on earth but instantly
kicked myself for throwing away my chance

at glory. Where? Why, there in the hereafter
I might never again come close to even
knocking on the door of, let alone
find myself feeling almost at home

in the next world. As it is, I'll always be
forever grateful for this new knowledge.

WORLDS APART

Today I sat down to Thanksgiving dinner
with you & my two boys, the three faces
my heart called forth & set before my eyes
not even six months ago when I stood

to step into the afterlife, feeling
for real the peace that passes understanding,
but couldn't tear myself away from, say,
sitting around our kitchen table here

in Lincoln on the fourth Thursday, as Lincoln
decreed, of the eleventh month & talking
turkey (not to mention gobbling it up!)
again with you & both my kids as now,

I who (thank God) lived to see my prayers
answered, not in the next life but in this.

HOMESICK FOR HERE

When I went & died the fourth & last time,
I didn't ride into the sunset but climbed
a Jacob's ladder of clouds to end up

facing the same blue-&-gold horizon
I saw driving my boy to school this morning
at sunup. There he sat, one of the three

reasons (along with you & his big brother)
I stepped back from the bottom line instead
of entering, amazingly, the Kingdom
of Heaven, on the threshold as I stood

of the Promised Land. Little did he know
that I'd returned to take the same old roads
& see the same old sun rise yet again
every last day now as if for the first time.

LATE REVELATION

The first day I could tell my sons apart,
fifteen years between them though there are,
I was at least a lost week out from open-
heart surgery but, I knew, in my right mind

at last. I had confused them with each other
over & over, even as they stood
side by side before me in the days
immediately after I emerged

from the worst of my travails & got asked
who was who, in the face of their disbelief,
to test how far I'd come on my way back
to myself. *Listen,* I told them, *God is real—*

I'm living proof! Despite my urgency,
those two rolled their eyes at their crazy father.

WELCOME TO ASIA

I. Flying Turkish Airlines to My Son's Wedding

All the folk wisdom I've learned I acquired
in Turkey, where I happen to be flying
yet again tonight but now with the blessing
of a new moon, which Turks remain convinced
proves auspicious for beginning long journeys
& undertakings of great magnitude.

As if on cue, the captain breaks the news
my taxiing Airbus has been directed
to go back to the gate we have just left,
in order to correct a "technical
problem" he calls "small," as if such a thing
could ever be minor when it comes to jets.

"Minor" is forgetting my lucky blue
Pilot gel pen back in Security
& having to press my point here instead
with this ball point, a "Souvenir of Boston,"
when I remember I can also wish
upon the same crescent moon as if praying,

& in no time I find myself airborne,
keeping an eye in time on Georgia O'Keeffe's
heaven-sent striations of pink & orange
running parallel to those of gold
& azure above the gray horizon line—
abstractions made concrete, a new day rising.

II. International Arrivals

When I showed my face after so many hours,
I must have truly been a sight for sore eyes,

considering my son had long devoted
himself to seeing that I saw this day

in Istanbul by doing all he could
last summer to make sure that I survived

coming back from the dead more than once,
determined as he was I'd be the first

father to live to witness a son married
in three generations of his family.

I hugged my son & air-kissed, Euro-style,
his future bride when I arrived, his mission

accomplished in a good six months: my legs
back under me at last, my heart new-fangled.

III. Ceremony at the Pera Palace

My room comes complete with a fainting couch,
a decorating touch appropriate

to the late-Victorian Era, when this grand
hotel opened its doors first to the rich

& famous of its day. Today it hosts
Asians in the main, but thirty-five years

ago I said good-bye (& good riddance)
to such a sorry-assed, down-at-the-heels

establishment as had seen better days,
a legend past its prime. Back with my younger

son to see his thirty-something brother
wed here tomorrow at the age my father

got married, too, off to Asia himself
(the Far East, not the Near), I find the place

glowing like a bride now, each chandelier
a blizzard of lights in each hall of mirrors.

IV. Epithalamion (for John & Melis)

At last you can stop living for yourselves
& start to live for each other, without
losing track of who you are but, with luck,
finding your true calling in finding love
& putting each other's happiness first,
before your own—no, not one or the other
of you but both. So what if you end up
falling all over yourselves or bend over
backwards to make each other happy? Being
on the same page, you'll never work at cross-
purposes but always experience
the heavenly feeling you're both of one mind,
hearts beating as one & wanting whatever
the other desires. For instance, a good bi-
national couple like you must love each
other's native land as much as your own.
I mean, fifty years ago I stepped off
the Orient Express in Istanbul
without a clue that I would come to love
Turkey so deeply I'd spend the next fifty
or so summers here. Now, at the winter
solstice, I congratulate you: unlike
poor Edmund Spenser, who rued marrying
on the shortest night of the year, you've smartly
made the longest your own wedding night.

V. Bringing the Underworld to Light

Before my son tied the knot yesterday,
his bride's father smashed a pomegranate

on the pavement behind his daughter's green
Mini, as she was driven from his house

on the Asian side & crossed the Bosporus
to the Palace, where she'd get dressed for the night

of ceremony ahead. Pomegranates,
bursting as they are with blood-red seeds,

have long stood for fertility, for reasons
too obvious to mention, & have been called

"love-apples"; his gesture thus beseeched
such goddesses as still rule Asia Minor

to grant him grandkids by the power of love
I fathomed when, for the first time this evening,

I tasted the true sweetness of those seeds
in season here now in the dead of winter.

VI. Christmas in Istanbul

Here where I've always been an infidel,
I'm back this year a new believer, after

meeting my end but seeing it reversed,
& reappear now where I first arrived

from Paris half a century ago
to fly Aegean Jet, the cut-rate midnight

bus to Izmir I took my life in my hands
getting on & corkscrewing down the winding

coastal road there in the dark, hell-bent
on reaching it by morning. Through the din

of Turkish music played for me, the driver's
first American passenger, the gold

script on the green banner above his head
told anyone else too scared to sleep

to trust in Allah. Come this far today,
I must have been in God's hands even then.

VII. Subway

Fast approaching the middle of his life,
my son led me through the Underground
in Istanbul toward the end of mine,
like Aeneas hauling his old man through hell.

Thus he began returning here the favor
I did him when I held his hand through Turkey
his first fifteen summers, much as this morning
he climbed with me, step by step, through the fifteen
centuries the Galata Tower has stood.

Now the future lies with him, only three
days married though he is, while at my age
I have to watch the number of cheap Swatches
that I collect, lest I run out of time
to wear them all before I wear out, too.

VIII. Postscript

Outside my window on my Turkish Air
flight home from my son's wedding, the North Star

appeared so close it filled the glass, a white-
hot rock of ice in my face courtesy

of the curvature of Einstein's universe.
My Airbus had arced north toward the Arctic

Circle, its flight plan following the shape
of the globe instead of mistaking a straight

line for the shortest distance between two points.
But as the crow flies, I have seen the last

of the black hole I came from, the well I kept
going back to for as long as I could.

As a rule, though, the world throws us a curve
as a matter of course, & here it is

already, the last day of the dark year
I saw the light—or what I took to be.

THE SNOW MAN

Deep in the heart of January, heartless
though it is, you once more commemorated
our first date, now seventeen years ago

to the day, with roses of the same number
as orange as Satsuma tangerines
in season again or as the rising sun

the moment that it bubbled into view
above the horizon, a regular ball
of fire dripping light, when I drove our boy

to school this morning at daybreak. Sixteen
in March, he shaved today for the first time,
he told me as he said good-night, & all

his days to come I'd never live to see
flashed before my eyes here in two-faced
January, when I looked backward, too,

& saw the ball that you & I got rolling
there in the dead of a winter long gone
snowballed, before we knew it, into a man.

FEBRUARY IS FOR THE BIRDS

1. Questionable Language

Fitful, colorless birds I can't ID
tsk-tsk me to beat the band as they flit

among the bare branches of the lilac
outside my door. I know its name because

I can remember when it last had leaves—
heart-shaped, in fact, as though at once recalling

& heralding Valentine's Day (today),
giving me the heart to weather the months

until Memorial Day, when I'll salute
my heart on its first anniversary

of cheating death. For now, these meaningless,
nondescript birds all keep wagging their tongues,

trying to shame me, so to speak, for not
knowing the name of every last fellow

resident on God's soon-to-be green earth,
chiding me for my human uselessness.

2. Twitter Feed on Presidents' Day

Any number of white-throats in a feeding
frenzy *tweet-tweet* incessantly inside

my leafless hedge on the first, of all things,
summer day in February. Last

summer I couldn't climb in or out
of my own house under my own power,

my legs left weakened by my weeks in bed
that gave my opened-&-shut heart a breather.

The sudden change of weather quickens even
the pulses of these random sparrows found

(& heard) flocking together at lunch time.
It's been fifty-five years this month my father

—a druggist's son done in by Inderal—
lost his pulse in the OR I sped down

Excelsior Boulevard toward too late
in Brother Patrick's blue, school Malibu.

HARD SPRING

> *In the juvescence of the year*
> *Came Christ the tiger.*
> T. S. Eliot

1
The new moon sets like a skiff going under
black-&-blue water, my hopes & fears
sinking back to the bottom of the dark

night of my soul they sprang from. Wait, I almost
forgot: spring begins tomorrow, at least
according to the calendar, if nothing

else; in fact, one forecast I read wrote spring
off this year—"Gone missing!" it said. Who cares?
This time around, I'll celebrate my own

rebirth as much as Mother Earth's, here still
despite such odds against me as my doctor
broke down for me at my check-up today—

"A miracle!" he said. Far from selling
spring short, I'm speaking its truth from my heart:
Going through hell proved my chance of a lifetime.

2
Good Friday, of all days, marks the appearance
in my backyard of the season's first crocus
risen from the dead ground with flying colors—

the purple, in fact, of Lenten flags flown
to this day outside St. Jude's down the road—
affirming my belief at once in heaven

& earth. I've learned my lesson my first spring
back from the dead myself last summer, when
I saw the light—dawn on a higher plane—

yet longed, deep in my heart, for one more shot
here at this level, where the thrill of life
comes & goes by the minute, day to day.

As close as I came to time without end,
I still take sanctuary in the present
& love living for these moments of change.

3
Native Americans believed the world
rested on the back of a great turtle;
me, too. I've come here every day of Holy

Week to see if I could spot a turtle
sunning itself on a tree fallen across
the Blackstone River I still walk beside

religiously. This morning, on the eve
of Easter, three green turtles stuck their necks
out & revealed their orange underbellies.

I never should have seen another spring
who came back from the dead a good four times
after ascending, once, to the next world.

The afterlife began when I returned
to this & learned, rehabbed by "Minnesota"
Max, to walk again as if reborn.

www.ingramcontent.com/pod-product-compliance
Lightning Source LLC
Chambersburg PA
CBHW020627300426
44112CB00010B/1232